Furtive Nudist

KEN CAMPBELL is well known to television audiences for his portrayal of Fred Johnson, Alf Garnett's neighbour in *In Sickness and in Health*. In 1976 he founded the Science Fiction Theatre of Liverpool where he directed two monumental epics: the twenty-two hour cult show *The Warp* and *Illuminatus!*, which was chosen to open the Cottesloe at the National Theatre in London. He also founded the legendary *Ken Campbell's Roadshow*. He is the author of such children's plays as *Old King Cole*, *Skungpoomery*, *School for Clowns*, *Clowns on a School Outing* and *Frank 'n' Stein*, plus books for two musicals: *Bendigo* and *Walking Like Geoffrey*. His film scripts have included *Unfair Exchanges*, which starred Julie Walters and *The Madness Museum*, in which Ken Campbell played the Proprietor of the asylum.

'Ken Campbell's one-man show is a mixture of autobiographical ramble, ego-trip without chips, and evocation of a strange alternative England of teleportation and trepanning. But it has a compelling fascination, as if one were being button-holed for two-and-a-half hours by a mixture of Ken Dodd and the Ancient Mariner. Essentially, Mr Campbell is a born yarn-spinner who finds mysterious connections between everything. . . .'

Michael Billington *The Guardian*

Ken Campbell

FURTIVE NUDIST

Drawings by Eve Stewart

Methuen Drama

First published in Great Britain in 1992 by Methuen Drama,
Michelin House, 81 Fulham Road, London SW3 6RB
and distributed in the USA by HEB Inc., 361 Hanover Street,
Portsmouth, New Hampshire NH 03801-3959.

A CIP catalogue record for this book
is available from the British Library
ISBN 0 413 66100 8

Cover photograph of Ken Campbell by Aedan Kelly

Caution
All rights in this text are strictly reserved and application for
performance etc. should be made to Peters, Fraser and Dunlop Ltd,
5th Floor, The Chambers, Chelsea Harbour, Lots Road, London
SW10 0XF.
No performance may be given unless a license has been obtained.

Photoset by Deltatype Ltd, Ellesmere Port, Cheshire
Printed in England by
Clays Ltd, St Ives plc

The voice had spoken to me, reminding me of
the place to which Horselover Fat had gone.
In his search. . . As we had been told, originally,
long ago, to do; I kept my commission.

Philip K. Dick
Valis

Furtive Nudist

Furtive Nudist
An Epic

Furtive Nudist is a development of
The Recollections of a Furtive Nudist
which was directed by Gillian Brown at the Offstage
Downstairs, Camden Town, 21 June 1988.
Performed as an oral work by Ken Campbell
from 1988 to 1991 in England – Scotland – Wales –
Eire – Newfoundland – New York – Chicago – Amsterdam

Produced by Colin Watkeys

ONE

I was born in the early part of the war —
in London —
(Ilford actually) —
(Actually I was *conceived* as a result of the War —
my parents had long wanted a child —
but nothing was happening for them on that front —
then one night a low-flying doodle-bug over Ilford *whoooshes*
    the relevant juices into my formation) —
My earliest memories are of being under the dining-room
    table —
with my Mum —
(the table had a sheet of heavy metal on top of it) —
sometimes my Dad joining us —
and after the banging and the whizzing —
the silence —
only the sound of your own ears —
and then the 'All Clear' siren —
and I'm put into the toilet —
'To perform', they say —
And I think I may have given my best performances in there.

I used to perform for the creatures I fancied I could see in the
    lino —
old orange lino with that multi-coloured abstract patterning —

but I could divine swamps and jungles —
and the creatures —
very particularly the FROG —
bulging eyes —
no lips —
insistent, demanding smile —
it's the Frog who draws from me these extraordinary
    performances —
and not just performances —
sensational plotlines —
('Flying Bomb Riders of Africa', 'Christmas with the Red
    Indians') —
Also the Frog sometimes emanated a form of Knowledge —
encoded in rhythmic reiteration:
'In Ma a Roonoo-ko —
In Ma a Roonoo-ko —
In Ma a Roonoo-ko' —
and often delivered so forcefully it could still be received under
    the table —
some distance from the bathroom —
'In Ma a Roonoo-ko' —
Sometimes it was comforting to know that —
on other occasions just a little alarming.

— ❓ —

Something else —
I had a partner —
As I recall it —
TWO OF US SAT THERE.

— ❓ —

In his novel *Valis* the American author Philip K. Dick writes
    about his *alter ego* —

and he calls this *alter ego* 'Horselover Fat' —
A recent Philip K. Dick Society Newsletter reminds us how he
    came up with that name —
'Philip' in the Greek means 'admirer of the equestrian arts' —
and 'Dick' is the German for 'fat' —
HORSELOVER FAT —
If I do that with my name:
'Kenneth' in the Celtic means 'the handsome one' —
'Camp'? —
'Bell'? —
PRETTYBOY TENTRINGER —
So that's how I'll refer to my colleague of the lost toilet dramas:
Prettyboy Tentringer.

When I was eight (the war now well over) I was allowed to join
    the State Barkingside Saturday Morning Pictures Club —
There was a theory that if you could pitch an ice-cream tub just
    right you could get it to slide down the projector beam and hit
    the screen —
But only John Spooner had ever done it —
Waves of mass attempts to emulate John Spooner's feat would
    punctuate the proceedings —
One Saturday John Spooner got us all to bring a jam-jar of foul
    concoction of our own devising in to the cinema and take
    them (hidden under our jerseys) up into the circle —
During the Tex Ritter feature we all made hideous puke noises and
    emptied the jars onto the stalls.

Sadly John Spooner was to be very badly injured —
He'd brought along a box of matches and under the cinema
    seats was holding the Set Light to Your Farts Olympics —

and he set light to his trousers —
and had to have his arsehole grafted with a bit of his elbow.

Soon as we're turned out of the State, a regular bunch of us mob
    up the road to the Fairlop Aerodrome —
this is a disused military airfield with swampy, stinky
    underground tunnels —
old gun turret bunker things called pillboxes —
and one Saturday word goes round that there's a German in one
    of the pillboxes —
we know our duty —
we go to rout him out —
dozen or so kids —
and there he is in the pillbox —
a little weaselly man and he's protecting some pages he's been
    writing —
and we chase him out —
we chase him right off the airfield —
and then we go back to that pillbox —
examine his pages —
and yes they are written in foreign —
and we pee on them —
we have a good group wee on them —
(which was all done quite decently: first of all us eight lads do
    our business on them and then the girls are sent in).

But something about that —
the next week I return to the pillbox —
alone —
the German's not been back —

his yellowing pages —
I turn them over —
with a stick —
(the link between Germans and germs was well known at that
    time) —
and amongst the writing I find his drawings —
really terrific drawings —
of Red Indians —
there was 'Winnetou' the Red Indian Chief, and the young
    brave, 'Appanatshka' and —
(this one lovingly detailed) —
the beautiful Red Indian Squaw Princess 'NSCHO-TCHI'.

— ? —

From the bit I've had to do with the bringing up of my daughter
    I can confirm this:
young kids produce 'sticky' naturally —
they haven't necessarily been playing in the jam —
at times of excitement they just produce the stuff —
exude it —
this sticky —
and when I decided (at that moment of the decision) to take
    home the picture of Nscho-Tchi —
I exuded a load of it —
A record amount.

— ? —

But I was aware of twin health hazards here:
1. It was a German's —
2. It had been peed on —
and the portrait of Nscho-Tchi was not to survive its long soak in
    scalding Pine and Harpic water —

(except in memory —
I can recall it clearly to this day —
in all its detail).

When I was 25 the phone rang —
It was my father —
he'd now retired —
he and my stepmother (my mother died when I was 12) had
    gone to live in Croyde, North Devon —
he wanted to know if I was ever going to visit them —
? —
'Yes', I said, 'I'll come now'.

—❓—

A35 van I had then —
and rounding the coastal bends, almost at Croyde, on the left,
    Saunton Sands —
a dunescape —
one is minded of the Moon —
I parked the van and set off over the Moon —
It was peculiarly hot that day —
(it was early Feb.) —
I returned to the van —
I hadn't thought to bring my trunks —
but I was stripping off —
down to my underpants —
(even right back in those days I always wore the 'boxer' style of
    underpant —
it was due to an article I'd read) —
and thus un-attired I was back over the dunes —

and the dunes and I were one —
and then I was addressed by a disembodied voice.

And the Voice said: 'Why've you got your underpants on?' —
I said: 'Well . . . for decency' —
and the Voice said: 'But there's nobody about' —
? —
and I said: 'Yes, well, for sure we can't see anybody but
    somebody might pop up at any moment' —
'No', said the Voice, 'You've got your underpants on because
    you're scared to take them off.'

Scared? —
Really? —
I wasn't scared of being arrested —
winding up in the Police Station —
I rather felt the tale you could tell afterwards would make it
    worth it —
so —
it was Dad —
I was very fond of that bloke —
and to be arrested for an antic like this just round the corner
    from where he'd just moved to —
No.

So —
What I did —
I took down my underpants literally CIRCUMSPECTLY —

making sure, round 360 degrees, that I was unobserved —
and then I buried the pants under a bush —
and I took pains to MEMORIZE THAT BUSH —
and then I set off.

— ? —

Did you ever see Kurosawa's classic movie *Seven Samurai*? —
Remember how they run in it? —
Not like joggers —
they run knees bent and arse low —
(well they want to keep their bollocks out of the way of the
    arrows) —
and that's how I was —
low bush to little grass clump to low bush —
and suddenly overhead the ENEMY! —
THE AIR-SEA RESCUE HELICOPTER! —
I drop where I am —
cover my crime with sand —
but it occurs to me:
those guys are going to think something's up if they see me in
    the middle of this desolate duneworld building sandcastles —
they're going to think I'm an idiot in need of rescuing —
so I posed as a boffin almost at the conclusion of some algebraic
    conundrum I was working out in the sand —
'Unified field theory! —
Almost there —
if you'd just fuck off!' —
and they pass overhead —
and on.

— ? —

And up again and on —
in fits and spurts —

the Samurai —
aware round 360 degrees —
high sandbank to bush to clump —
and now I've come to the end of the Dunes and I'm faced with
    the challenge of the Great Plain.

— ? —

Wide open space now —
no cover —
a Canyon —
and I'm crouched behind the last bush and I feel great and I'll
    tell you who I am, I am Winnetou in his prime and it's not a
    question of WHETHER I'm going to take on the Challenge
    of the Canyon it's just a question of WHEN and the answer to
    When is when the juices are UP and the juices are UP and
    I'm over the Canyon and listen I have recall of FLYING over
    some parts of that terrain and I get a flash of who's going to
    be over there when I get there:
NSCHO-TCHI —
Nscho-Tchi is in them woods!

— ? —

But Nscho-Tchi had gone —
(there were signs she'd been there) —
it was getting cold —
I decided to go back.

— ? —

Re-traversing the Great Plain I just strolled —
it seemed to me it was now mine, this territory —

and that's when I was seen —
way up aloft, a man walking his dog, he saw me —
and I just turned fully to him and waved.

And then back on the dunes —
and I thought 'Yeah that was a bright thing to do' (now
    samuraiing low) 'he's going to race round with that big dog
    and make a citizen's arrest' —
but clump, bush, dune and I've samuraied myself back to the
    well-remembered bush and pants now back on —
Wheee —
back in the van —
wheee —
Very nice my Dad's new place.

And that night at my Dad's I had a dream —
(in certain company I have referred to it as a vision) —
anyway, in this dream, I understood Everything —
What we're all doing here —
The Grand Purpose, the Whole Show —
What we're meant to do —
What I was meant to do —
I thought, Fuck this is important —
so I woke myself up.

And by the bedside was a book of crank speculation by a couple
    of Frenchmen —

(A couple of Frogs!) —
Louis Pauwels' and Jacques Bergier's *The Dawn of Magic* —
And I wrote on to the page it was opened at (page 98), all it
   seemed to me that would be necessary to reconjure the vision.

— ❔ —

Next morning I read what I'd written:
'ENORMOUS SWIMMING BATH
VEGETATION AND FOLIAGE IN IT'

— ❔ —

It wasn't enough! —
Why had I made no mention of the GEEZER? —
Yes that was the location, enormous swim bath of vegetation,
   but there'd been this geezer down there, the all-important
   geezer, and it was from him, presumably, I'd learnt . . .
what I'd now utterly forgotten —
And the more I tried to recall him —
the more it seemed that the act of recollection itself was driving
   him into the mists —
and Fog.

— ❔ —

It was a couple of days later (still in Croyde) that a relative of
   my stepmother comes to stay —
and I'd not met him before —
and he was a great old soldier —
he'd been in Yalta in 1945 with Churchill, Roosevelt and
   Stalin —

he'd drunk Stalin under the table —
and it was very late now, there was just him and me up —
and he was telling me the most appalling military secrets —
and we got through a whole bottle of whiskey —
EACH —
(Let me warn you about that last inch and a half of a bottle of
    whisky —
if it's not you who's doing the talking —
I think it might be damn near fatal) —
I was able to get out of the room with dignity —
but once I was in the corridor I knew it was medically advisable
    to CRAWL —
And I crawled to my room on the ground floor —
and I lay on the bed and the ceiling was swinging into the
    wall —
and I knew I'd done it this time —
this was permanent! —
And then I heard from the Voice.

— ❓ —

And the Voice said: 'Well you know what to do!' —
And I said: 'What NOW!?' —
(it was about half past two in the morning) —
and I'm looking out of the window and it does seem that
    everyone else is asleep —
certainly their lights are all out —
there's just the square of light on the lawn coming from my
    room.

— ❓ —

So —
I took all my clothes off —

and hopped out through the window —
and I skirt the square of light —
and I edge along the hedge —
and then I think I may have left my body for a few moments
   because I have vivid recollection of the sight of my own bare
   arse as I open the gate of my Father's new house —
and step out into the road.

A NAKED MAN IN A COUNTRY ROAD —
and heading towards Croyde Village —
but so Awake! —
so Aware! —
the slightest sound that might have been the footfall of a
   distantly oncoming pedestrian:
first glint over the brow of headlights:
I dive through the hedge into the field behind —
I flatten myself in the ditch —
uncaring of the scratches, the stings, the cuts —
the muck —
in fact delighting in it! —
and now I'm coming into the village itself —
and it's somewhat lamplit —
(there's a mist, but not a helpful mist,
it's a theatrical mist, a Macbeth mist —
creates mood but only comes up to your knees —
no Samurai could crouch that low —
a limbo dancer, maybe, but a skill that, not mine) —
and houses now and folk who live atop the shops.

Best thing to do (it occurs to me) is to make myself
   IMPOSSIBLE OF ASPECT —

My Dad used to take me to the Crazy Gang Shows —
(Flannagan and Allen, Naughton and Gold, etc) —
and there was a bit of visual grammar peculiar to their shows:
if a Gang member's arsehole was touched up by a ladder, a
    rake, whatever, if he backed into the banisters —
this would trigger him into his own personal goosed-spesh
    eccentric walk —
and it was in a manner inspired by those memories, the Ministry
    of Funny Walks, Professor Walloffski, the Royal Ballet —
and my own nightmares —
that I progressed myself through Croyde Village.

My reasoning was this:
If someone came to their window, *Aghah!* yawned, saw me —
! —
They'd assume they were still asleep.

And now I'm outside the last shop in Croyde —
and it's the only interesting shop in Croyde —
it's the Shell Shop which sells the local and foreign shells —
and I have the courage (a light drizzle now) to linger at the Shell
    Shop window and pick my favourite exhibit:
the shell frog.

And then on and a left turn and down past the caravans and
    onto the beach —
and on the beach I hear voices —

and I fancy these are of the bodied variety and so I give them a
    wide berth, and then I'm at the sea, and I have a sensible
    swim in the sea —
(bracing how the salt bites into the wounds I'd received in the
    hedgerows) —
and out of the sea and across the wide beach and up the cliff
    walk this time and over the road —
and hop back in through the window —
and the Voice says: 'OK now?'

— ❓ —

And the only answer I could give was:
'I've never in my life felt better.'

— ❓ —

And I told no-one of these things for many years —
But then I was in Frankfurt, in the Café Fundus, and I'm
    drinking Himbiergeist in iced glasses with an artist called
    Hans —
and I tell him —
and then Hans tells me his story:
Three years previously (Hans telling me his story) he'd been
    living in the South of Germany in the small town of Pee —
'Of PEE!?' —
and then I realized what he was doing —
in the manner of Thomas Hardy and Edgar Allan Poe he was
    giving me the initial letter of the place (not 'Pee' but
    'P____') —
but I'd never heard anyone TALK like that —
'So you're living in P____, Hans?' —
(What secrets now?)

— ❓ —

Hans had a studio in P____ —
and he'd set himself a courageous artistic challenge —
he'd stitched canvas together to the exact dimensions of the
    Bayeux Tapestry —
but not to knit and sew us something, no —
he was an oil painter, surreal, science-fictional —
and here's how he was going about it:
every night at midnight he'd step out from his studio and he'd
    walk the streets of P____, he'd walk 'em and walk 'em, for
    hours, till it comes to him which part of the mighty canvas he
    is to attack that night, and then he returns to the studio and
    paints through the night until his vision is completed or he
    falls apart exhausted —
and then the next night's prowl round P____.

— ❓ —

And it's early morning hours and Hans is out round P____ and
    he hears from the Voice and the Voice says to Hans:
'Move the stones' —
and Hans doesn't understand the instruction and it comes again:
    'Move the stones' —
and this time Hans is outside someone's front garden and there
    is a large and curious rock in there and perhaps it wants
    moving —
and he scrabbles it up and once he's got it in his arms IT'S
    TELLING HIM WHERE IT WANTS TO GO —
and it's round the corner and in someone else's garden —
and he's about to go and then he hears from another stone —
and that's what he's doing now, every night round P____ —
HE'S MOVING THE STONES.

— ❓ —

Sometimes he's merely twisting them —
turning them, re-pointing them in situ —
other times he's devoting a whole night to one stone's
   considerable journey —
(For particularly large rocks which required a distant relocating
   he would use his niece's pram.)

And it's all having magic effect on the mighty opus —
things are moving apace on the great canvas —
and then he's picked up for it by the Polizei of P____.

Ach so and *und so weiter* and its turns out that stone moving
   isn't much of a crime —
but for Hans's own protection it's felt that he should now turn
   his talents toward jig-saws and basket-weaving in a supervised
   environment —
and he's in this place four weeks and then he's called up to see
   the 'Fat Important Man' —
And the Fat Important Man takes a deal of interest in Hans and
   his art and his ideas and his life and then there's a long pause
   and the Fat Important Man goes out comes back in with a big
   cigar and fools around cutting it and lighting it and then he
   asks Hans this:
'Have you a commission?'

The question asked in conspiratorial tones —
What is he really asking? —

The Fat Important Man? —
('Have you a commission?')
Hans didn't know —
but he answered: 'Yes'.

— ❓ —

And the Fat Important Man bows slightly and he apologizes to
    Hans that he's been kept in there so needlessly and so long —
and he helps Hans pack —
and he waves Hans onward with his 'commission' and wishes
    him all the best —
But when Hans gets back to his studio, he decides to remove
    himself forever from the small town of P___ —
and go live in the large city of F___.

— ❓ —

TWO

Have you a commission? —
HAVE YOU A COMMISSION? —
The way Hans reported it I'd found it stirring —
Have you a commission? —
in any event it's a good tip —
If you're ever in that circumstance and the guy asks you if
    you've got a commission say YES! —
But handy if you actually had one —
If I were ever to have one it would surely have something to do
    with the Dream:
'ENORMOUS SWIMMING BATH
VEGETATION AND FOLIAGE IN IT' —
(Imagine this: one night, in a dream, the Bard of Avon hits on
    his finest so far and wakes himself up and supposes himself to
    be quilling down the necessary notes of the vision —
Next morning he reads what he's written:
'CASTLE
SCANDINAVIA
BLOKE IN TIGHTS'.)

— ❓ —

And page 98 —
(*The Dawn of Magic*) —
just above where I wrote 'Enormous swimming bath etc.' —
this (a quotation):

'I have spent much time thinking about the alleged pseudo-
relations that are called coincidences. What if some of them
should not be coincidences?' —
turning back a few pages to find who said that —
Charles Fort —
an American author of the twenties and thirties —
who'd written 'The crack-pot's *Golden Bough*' —
he was:
'One of the monstrosities of literature' —
'To read Charles Fort is like taking a ride on a comet' —
'Sends you reeling against the doors which open onto something
other' —
but Pauwels and Bergier had only read one book by Charles
Fort, *The Book of the Damned* —
in a footnote on page 95 they tell us another they've heard of —
LO! —
they'd heard that really was fantastic —
so this was the tip then —
towards my commission —
Get *LO!*

— ? —

I went to Foyle's and they were no bleedin' use at all —
Second-hand bookshops now —
Specialists in the Arcane —
London and environs —
and it's not till I get to Birmingham that I meet a man who's
heard of it —
and it's not till I get to Newcastle-upon-Tyne that I meet a man
who reckons he once had one —
and years are passing —
and I've given up the hunt —
and then I'm asked to direct a Canadian Comedy show —
and I'm in Toronto.

— ? —

And I'm trying to cast the thing —
and I'm not finding it easy —
I'm beginning to think that 'Canadian Comedy Show' might be a
    contradiction in terms —
(like 'Military Intelligence') —
and then one morning comes in this young tubby
    Newfoundlander, Andy Jones, and he had thick glasses that
    made his eyes look bulgy like a frog's, and he was funny, and
    I thought: 'We're OK now; just build the show round Andy
    Jones' and that afternoon I'm in the W. H. Smith's of
    Toronto —
and this is how it happened:
I was attracted by a large format book of old sepia photographs
    of Red Indians, taken in the 1880s, but it was up high, too
    high for me, and so I moved a cardboard box over to stand
    on, and my foot slipped and ripped open the box —
and inside were *Complete Works*es of Charles Fort.

— ❓ —

I am holding the treasure —
I allow it to open where IT will —
I read —
how —
Ladies! —
If you kiss a frog —
and make a regular practice of this —
(morning and evening I think was the recommended regimen
    here) —
and if the frog starts to look a bit dicky you must choose the
    most robust of his tadpoles and get kissing that —
And if you feel that soon you may be departing this vale of
    tears —

you must pass the practice on to your daughter —
and so it must go —
on through the generations —
the centuries —
but in the end —
says Fort —
YOU WILL COME UP WITH A PRINCE.

— ❓ —

And Fort's pseudo proof of this is a cup of tea:
Is not the tea at the very edge of the cup slightly more cuppish
    than the stuff in the middle? —
And is not the interior of the cup not a load more teaish than
    the outer part and the handle? —
Well, damn right, and I bought the book —
but, something about it, that book, and I didn't open it again
    while I was in Canada —
put it safely in my case —
and eventually back to London with it —
and still unopened further I put it pride of place on the
    bookshelf.

— ❓ —

And I also brought back with me Andy Jones because I thought
    people might like to laugh at him over here.

— ❓ —

My feelings about thinking at this time (1972) —
I held there to be a difference between 'I think' and 'it occurs to
    me that . . .' —

Thinking is a step by step affair —
Whereas —
'It occurs to me that . . .' —
Well sometimes the most extraordinary things may, unbidden,
  occur.

— ❓ —

And it was late one night and something was unbidden
  occurring —
and it was coming in in the form of an epic dramatic poem —
and I was writing it down as it came in and it was looking really
  good and I knew all I had to do was KEEP OUT OF THE
  WAY! —
and it had a curious set-up to it:
it was set in 1948/49 in the Dagenham/Chadwell Heath area —
and the heroes were these two guys and I think one of them was
  an ex-prisoner of war who'd not returned at the time of
  repatriation, and his younger mate, a young Dagenham lad,
  and these two were so into Red Indian culture that —
well they were unemployable —
but they'd developed interesting abilities —
they could decide their next action by reading cigarette
  smoke —
sometimes they'd go to the station in order to listen to the
  babblings of the winos and the shopping-bag ladies in the
  belief that one time in the jabber they'd pick out a spirit
  message from Mighty Manitou —
and they were into litter-divination —
they would, as it were, I Ching litter bins —
'Close cover before striking' is an answer if you've asked the
  question —
'Keep Dry and Away From Children' —
sometimes a motto for the day like:
'Courage's bitter' —

(I recently saw a hoarding, I think it was advertising a new-style
  thinking men's magazine: 'Measure your Manhood Without a
  Ruler' —
I think they'd have liked that.)

— ❷ —

I'm going to bother you with the last short section of the epic
  dramatic poem as it was coming in —
This bit is called: 'THE COMING OF NSCHO-TCHI':

   'In the Tavern by the Tram-Stop
   Heroes on the dark fire-water'

(which is Guinness) —

   'One pint, two, then three and four
   "See the moon!" cries Appanatshka
   "Moon is twice as big as usual
   Sign that something big will happen
   Night of nights that moon portends!"
   In that instant comes a Lady
   Lady with the Long Black Hair
   "May I sit here" says the Lady
   Sits down on adjoining chair —
   Heroes speechless, stare in wonder
   Stare at Lady's long black hair —
   "Das ist Nscho-Tchi, Appanatshka!
   Das ist Nscho-Tchi ist ganz klar!"
   (*and as they stare at her three ectoplasmic*
   feathers rise up behind her head)
   Full of panic hunt the heroes
   Hunt for clues for what to do —
   Beer-mats, bottles, peanut packets —
   Nothing written what to do!
   Lady gripped by fit of shudders
   "Ooo" she cries, then "Agh" and "O" —

"My brothers brave I bring you blessings
But I feel funny; I must go!" —
Up she goes and out the door (*slam*)
Falls under a passing Tram—'

And sod it! – I wrote that last line! —
'Falls under a passing Tram' —
No she didn't do that —
I'd got in the way! —
and I'd shut off the transmission.

— ❷ —

I tried to put my mind back into the receptive state it had
    presumably been in when the stuff was coming through —
but all I got was one sentence —
'HE WENT FOR AN ICE-CREAM IN THE INTERVAL' —
(He went for an ice-cream in the interval?) —
Suddenly I understood the meaning of that sentence:
It was the last time we saw Father! —
(I'm a seven-year-old little girl and my name is Maisie) —
We'd gone for a family outing to the Cinema —
we'd seen the first feature and then we wanted ice-creams and
    Dad had gone off to get the ice-cream —
THE END —
We know no more! —
We never saw him again —
Often we think of Father —
o yes often! —
we're haunted by the fucker! —
Better if he'd died of a stroke —
than that —
HE WENT FOR AN ICE-CREAM IN THE INTERVAL.

— ❷ —

And so what does this mean apropos the Epic Poem? —
She doesn't fall under a tram she —
DISAPPEARS —
SHE VANISHES —
and the *Complete Works* of Charles Fort fell off the book shelf.

— ❓ —

And once I had it in my hand I knew what it was doing there! —
You know that bit about kissing frogs? —
I thought: 'I'll nick that!' —
I'll ring it a bit and use it as an invocation to Nscho-Tchi —
And then I thought this book has only ever been opened at that
    particular page and there must be predilection in the volume
    to open there again if only I can feel where it most wants to
    open.

— ❓ —

But it didn't open at the Frog-Kissing page —
in fact I'll tell you something weird:
I've now combed through the *Complete Works* of Charles Fort
    many times and —
THAT BIT ABOUT KISSING FROGS ISN'T IN IT —
This is what I found myself reading:
(Chapter 16 of *LO!*) —

> 'He walked around the horses.
> Upon Nov. 25 1809, Benjamin Bathurst, returning from
> Vienna, where, at the Court of the Emperor Francis, he
> had been representing the British Government, was in
> the small town of Perleberg, Germany. In the presence
> of his valet and his secretary, he was examining horses,
> which were to carry his coach over more of his journey

back to England. Under observation, he walked around
to the other side of the horses. He vanished.
For details see the *Cornhill Magazine*, pages 55–279.'

— ❓ —

And it's all coming in again —
and a fine invocation to Nscho-Tchi is dictated:

    ' "Long time we no see Nscho-Tchi
    Nscho-Tchi where are you today?
    We see you by the shining waters
    See you in your plumes and braid
    You who spoke the speech of chipmunks
    (As do all daughters of the Moon)
    You who bathed in laughing waters —
    Nscho-Tchi come and see us soon!
    You will know us tho' our feathers
    Lie in drawers most of the day —
    Now we only don the raiment
    Very hidden, private times —
    But, Nscho-Tchi you will know us —
    Enter soon our love-sent rhymes . . ." '

And then as before:

    'In the Tavern by the Tram-Stop
    Heroes on the dark fire-water
    "See the moon' Etc
    . . . "Night of nights that moon portends!"
    . . . comes a Lady
    Lady with the Long Black Hair . . .
    "May I sit here?" . . .
    (*three ectoplasmic feathers* . . .)
    . . . Nothing written what to do!
    Lady gripped by fit of shudders

"Ooo" she cries, then "Agh" and "O" —
"My brothers brave I bring you blessings
But I feel funny; I must go!"
Schwupps!
'*Mein Gott, sie ist verschwunden!*' —
She who was there now has gone —
Into thin air she has vanished
Teleported miles away . . .
She now appears in North Alaska
On the White Man's "Dawson Trail" . . .
Meanwhile in Tavern wail the heroes
Rend the room with shrieks of loss —
Worried waiter brings fire-water
Brings them crisps and rolls and nuts —
In snow-white froth of dark fire-water
Read they the sign of where she's gone . . .
In the night she freezes solid
Statue Queen in Land of Gold —
But colder still than lonely Ice-Queen
Are the hearts of our two heroes:
They were young men,
                              now they're old.'

— ❓ —

And then with the satisfaction that I'd helped something
    remarkable into the world, I retired to bed —
and there was a silence —
more than mere quiet —
a devouring silence —
the silence was devouring the creaks and bumps and ticks which
    are proper to the night —
it had eaten away, even, the sound of my own ears —
and in that silence my mind kept playing over and re-playing
    what seemed a somewhat singular event of the evening:

What was that bit? —
He went for an ice-cream in the interval —
and I'd deduced he'd disappeared and then so she doesn't fall
    under a tram, she vanishes, and then Fort falling off the book
    shelf (but Man! it hadn't 'fallen' off at all it had sailed off the
    book shelf as if KICKED BY A TINY FOOT!) —
so there must be – it's obvious – there must be – a —
non-physical entity —
a 'fairy' if you will —
whose special subject is 'Enchanted Vanishment' —
and she was so tickled that I was going to be writing on her
    subject that she'd given this helpful kick to things.

— ❓ —

And I asked myself this: 'Well then, Kenneth, do you think
    people ever do just . . . vanish?' —
And my answer was 'YES! I do' —
and then I thought: 'Yeah, and I bet it's when you're as clear as
    this about it YOU GO!' —
and then a worse thought: 'Yeah, and I bet it's when you think
    you're as clear as this about it that you THINK YOU'VE
    GONE.'

— ❓ —

Try to shake the idea out of my head —
think about where I might go on holiday —
but I can't fool it —
(what?) —
there's a demand —
(inside me? outside me? I don't know) —
that I devote full mind to Vanishment —
Try to fight it! —

Fill the mind with Abstract Blackness —
not easy —
(possibly not possible) —
Maybe if I can recall specific black items —
black shoes —
black stockings —
black bin bags —
black toy train —
AND I'M WINNING —
but then I'm aware that every orifice of my body —
(and I refer here too to secondary orifices —
the nipples, the button thing in the middle of the tum) —
all my orifices have become worms —
ALIEN WORMS WITH TEETH —
and bent on vigorous self-ingurgitation.

— ? —

With will —
I attempt to draw all this orificular aggravation away —
and into the centre of the MIND —
and then I knew —
why cultures world-wide —
and going back centuries —
have always held that with certain mental states —
the only answer is to —
BORE A HOLE IN THE HEAD.

— ? —

The following morning I rose late —
I could find no clothes that suited my mood so I put none on —
I devoted some hours to bizarre experimentation like finding out
    actually how long you could take to make a cup of coffee —

whether I could read the mail without opening the envelopes —
But later, sometime after three in the afternoon, I was at work.

— ❷ —

I'd taken the *Complete Works* of Charles Fort into the toilet —
Chapter 16 of *LO!*, I read on —
HE RAN INTO THE MILL —
'Chicago Tribune, Jan. 5, 1900 – "Sherman Church, a young
   man employed in the Augusta Mills (Battle Creek, Mich.) has
   disappeared. He was seated in the Company's office, when he
   arose and ran into the mill. He has not been seen since. The
   mill has been almost taken to pieces by the searchers, and the
   river, woods, and country have been scoured, but to no avail.
   Nobody saw Church leave town, nor is there any known
   reason for his doing so." '
Ambrose Bierce, author of the *Devil's Dictionary*
   disappeared —
Fort writes:
'I wonder whether Ambrose Bierce ever experimented with
   self-teleportation. Three of his short stories are of
   "mysterious disappearances". He must have been
   uncommonly interested to repeat so.' —
And on into Chapter 17:
'One is snoring along, amidst the ordinary marvels of dream-
   land – and there one is, naked, in a public place, with no
   impression of how one got there. I'd like to know what
   underlies the prevalence of this dream, and its
   disagreeableness, which varies, I suppose, according to one's
   opinion of oneself. I think that it is sub-conscious awareness
   of something that has often befallen human beings, and that
   in former times was commoner. It may be that occult
   transportations of human beings do occur, and that, because
   of their selectiveness, clothes are sometimes not included.' —
'Naked in the street – strange conduct by a strange man.' . . .

Early in the evening of January 6th (1914) – 'weather
bitterly cold – a naked man appeared, from nowhere that
could be found out, in High Street, Chatham.' And 'I have
records of six persons, who, between Jan. 14, 1920, and Dec.
9, 1923, were found wandering in or near the small town of
Romford, Essex, England, unable to tell how they got there,
or anything about themselves.'

— ❓ —

And 'bizarre arrival of things' —
Apport of objects —
and then it came to me —
(why had my mind blanked it out) —
it had only been less than three weeks before —
THE SAGA OF THE KEYS! —
About seven in the evening —
decide I'll got to the pub —
feel for keys —
can't find keys —
there's been trouble with keys before —
if I put my keys anywhere I put them in the kitchen drawer —
if they're not in my pants pocket they're in the kitchen
    drawer —
but they're not in the kitchen drawer —
not in my pants pocket and not in the kitchen drawer —
and not on the hook —
I'm hunting through the pockets of pants I haven't worn for a
    year —
two pairs of pants I don't even recognize —
and they're not in the kitchen drawer and they're not on the
    hook and not in the pants and they're not by the bed —
looking in jackets now —
perhaps I've become the sort of person who puts his keys in
    jackets —
Kitchen Drawer: No —
Hook: No —
By the Bed: No —

Mac—Overcoat —
No—No! —
and I'm back in front of the kitchen drawer again —
And I shriek at it:
FUCKING KEYS BE IN THERE —
!!! —
Thank you —
off to the pub.

— ? —

This is how *LO!* begins:
'A naked man in a city street – the track of a horse in volcanic
    mud – the mystery of reindeer's ears – a huge black form like
    a whale, in the sky, and it drips red drops as if attacked by
    celestial swordfishes – an appalling cherub appears in the
    sea —
Confusions.
Showers of frogs and blizzards of snails – gushes of periwinkles
    down from the sky —
The preposterous, the grotesque, the incredible – and why, if I
    am going to tell of hundreds of these, is the quite ordinary so
    regarded?'
Note Fort's use of the hyphen —
LO! has more hyphens than any book I know —
(although I may just top it in this one) —
and somewhere he tells us why:
It's Fort's opinion that everything in the Universe is linked with
    everything else —
so a Full Stop is a Lie —
Or a Hyphen coming straight at you.

— ? —

'An unclothed man shocks a crowd – a moment later, if nobody
    is generous with an overcoat, somebody is collecting

handkerchiefs to knot around him. A naked fact startles a meeting of a scientific society – and whatever it has for loins is soon diapered with conventional explanations . . . The Princess Caraboo tells of herself, a story, in an unknown language, and persons who were themselves liars have said that she lied, though nobody has ever known what she told . . . – and where Cagliostro came from, and where he went, are so mysterious that only historians say they know – . . . An onion and a lump of ice – and what have they in common?'
Is this any regular way to write a book? —
Not essay style is it —
not poem —
my feeling —
growing —
was —
INVOCATION.

And at that moment there's a knock at the door and I decide to
    answer it —
(drape myself in the dog's blanket) —
Two actors at the door, Mark Weill and David Stockton, and
    their first words are:
'Andy Jones has disappeared.'

I say, 'Come in' —
I say, 'I think something's trying to teach me something' —
and I don't let them speak —
and I give them each a piece of paper and a pen and I say to
    write down, independently, no conferring, exactly what they
    mean by —
ANDY JONES HAS DISAPPEARED.

And they'd been rehearsing Andy's show pub hours in the
  Falcon in the King's Cross area —
and they'd been turfed out at 3:20 and Andy had said that he
  had to go to the toilet —
and so he'd gone down into the public convenience —
Mark and David waiting for him at the top —
and quite a long time had gone by —
and so they'd gone down to hurry him up —
and when they'd got down there —
THERE WAS NO-ONE THERE.

— ❓ —

I say, 'Listen it's like I've been signed up for a course at the
  Invisible College,' and I tell them about falling under the
  tram, and going for an ice-cream at the interval, and Bathurst
  teleporting off from behind his horses, and the fairy kicking
  Fort off the book shelf, and Mark says:
'I think we should go to the Police.'

— ❓ —

And Ah! and that's a dilemma and Yes! I can see that the Police
  might help us find Andy but really, I'm sure of this:
if we go rushing off to the cops at this point I'm going to be
  crossed off the register of the Phantom Academy —
so I say, 'Let's just call the Prophet in first' —
And this was agreed to.

— ❓ —

The Prophet was an extraordinary guy who'd moved in up the
  road —

He styled himself 'Protean Synthesist' —
and if you asked him a question —
you know those Hindu Gods and Goddesses that have the extra
    arms coming out of their elbows, shoulders, wherever? —
well, if you asked the Prophet a question it was as if with his
    many arms he was reaching into remote and remarkable
    libraries of world culture —
(he'd be speed-reading locked grimoires on your behalf) —
and he'd always give you an answer that no-one else could —
and, Yes, he'd come right over.

— ❓ —

When I heard his knock I'm straight to the door —
I want to test him —
Will he be up to THIS occasion? —
I say: 'Prophet! Andy Jones has disappeared and we think it's a
    "round the horses" job' —
PROPHET: (MANY ARMS REACHING INTO REMOTE
    LIBRARIES) . . . Benjamin Bathurst? —
YES!—Prophet, you passed! and now unloading all on the
    Prophet:
Thinking, occurring, ice-cream, fairy;
LO!, keys, Invocation, Andy Jones; —
and Mark (freaking) says: 'What's going on!?' —
And the Prophet says: 'Boys, do you listen to nothing that I tell
    you? The real nature of the Universe is unknown and
    unknowable! – Your problem is that your World-Reality
    Picture is based on half-ingested Science! – These so-called
    Scientific Laws aren't laws at all! – They weren't given to
    some bearded Gent on a Mountain Top! – They're mere
    observations on how it usually goes! – There is only one word
    in the English language which approximates the true nature of

the Universe and that word is "OTHER"! – and every little
once in a while THE OTHER WILL MANIFEST and it's
good to be around at those times, because, if ye've the
courage – THERE MAY BE SOMETHING UP FOR
GRABS!' —
and Mark says: 'I think we should go to the Police.'

— ? —

'For sure,' (Prophet taking the case) 'we could go to the
Police – and what are we going to tell them? – What've we got
for them? – there's Kenneth's visit from the "Library Angel"
and it'll be our duty, will it not, to draw attention to the
bizarre synchronicity that Kenneth is reading what he holds to
be incantatory literature in his lav and teleports Andy Jones
out of his toilet – what else have we got to give them on which
to base their enquiries? —
and if we go in telling them these things —
I think we'll be all right —
I don't think we'll be arrested —
But I'm fucking sure we'll be put on a list.'

— ? —

And Mark says: 'Well let's go and look for him' —
'For sure, we can go and look for him,' says the Prophet,
    '. . . but statistically, in cases of bizarre removal, one is
    quicker to be united with the victim if one just goes severely
    about one's business; and then, if what we all hope happens,
    happens, that Andy Jones is returned to flesh-form in the
    Camden Town area, he'll have something to return to – you
    two,' (Mark and David) 'if you weren't here what would you
    be doing?' —

Mark said: 'Well we might be doing anything now, but in half an
hour we'd be rehearsing again' —
The Prophet said: 'So go rehearse.'

— ? —

And Mark and David went and I asked the Prophet this:
'Do you think what we have here with Andy Jones is an actual
case of "round the horses" teleportation?' —
And the Prophet said: '. . . No.'

— ? —

'No,' he said, 'what you've got here, I compute, is a case of
Invisibility!' —
'Invisibility?!' —
Apparently Invisibility is merely a matter of being able to hide
in front of things —
'How does that work?'
'I've told you, haven't I,' said the Prophet, 'about the
fourteenth-century Japanese Spy-Courier Monks?' —
'I dunno . . . you may have . . .' —
Evidently, an article in a recent *Lancet* had vindicated the early
work in this field by the fourteenth-century Japanese Spy-
Courier Monks – Experiments had been done on the eye-balls
of newly-hatched ducklings – and the muscles of their tiny
eye-balls had responded to the shape of PREDATORY birds
flying overhead, but had in no way responded to the shapes of
starlings, pigeons or Concorde —
'And as it was with the ducklings, so it is with us,' said the
Prophet —
'From the moment we are hatched from our mother's womb the
muscles of our eye-balls are ready, from that first moment, to
RESPOND TO THE SHAPE WHICH THREATENS –

thus – if you can train yourself to progress yourself in a
series of BIZARRELY UN-ALARMING POSTURES, you
can by-pass the muscles of the human eye . . .' —
And the Prophet waved me Goodbye —
With his many arms.

— ? —

And yet —
Isn't the Prophet there, (great man), explaining one miracle
   with two? —
Go back to Andy Jones in the public convenience —
in his cubicle —
finishing off —
now coming up the metal stairs —
Let's say he's 'adjusting his dress' and in so doing he happens to
   hit one of those bizarrely un-alarming postures thus
   by-passing the muscles of Mark and David's eye-balls! —
BUT THEN THEY TOO MUST HAVE BEEN LOLLING
   ABOUT IN BIZARRELY UN-ALARMING POSTURES
   WHICH BY-PASSED THE MUSCLES OF THE
   EYE-BALLS OF ANDY JONES! —
(I give you the Prophet's explanation —
it may give comfort to some —
I tell you this:
if you feel you may have been responsible for the teleportation
   of a treasured chum it gives you pause.)

— ? —

I wasn't to hear from the Voice for sixteen years —
(dating from the teleportation of Andy Jones) —
I'd found a lost bit of London —
(actually my dog found it) —

Only those who know it know it —
The Valley beneath Stamford Hill —
and the Abbey National and I bought a modest house there —
Step round the corner and onto the tow-path —
(Tow-path of the Navigation Cut of the River Lea) —
and do you believe you're in London, friend; look on the back
    of that old man's bike —
that wooden box on the back with a cabbage and some onions in
    it —
he's just picked them from his allotment! —
that's a heron! —
You just missed them but they were cormorants! —
(Tottenham's up to the left, we're walking to the right) —
passed my neighbours who live on the narrow boats —
the rowing club —
The Rowing Club Café —
also known as George's Café and it's been a caff for ninety
    years, and the first time I went inside I thought I was *déjà
    vu*ing:
it was a little like the club-house pavilion of the Valentine's
    Tennis and Social Club at Gants Hill —
and my Father had been secretary of that club when I was seven
    or so —
and George was selling those post-war cakes I hadn't seen for
    thirty or more years:
puff pastry jobs, with icing sugar on the top and noodles of
    coconut embedded in the icing-sugar, and something a wee bit
    sinister in the middle.

— ? —

And then I'd gone way back:
I was about seven, and I'm playing on the floor of the
    Valentine's Tennis Club Pavilion, and my Father's sitting at a
    table writing whatever it is he has to write in his enormous

ledger and there are only two other people in there, a male
member, beginning to bald, and he's teaching a new young
lady member how to play darts and he's exciting her with this
piece of information: 'You don't hold your dart like this as
you'd think', he's saying, showing his dart pointing towards
the board, 'but like this', point downwards, and he throws off
his three demonstration darts and goes to the board to
retrieve them, and the girl says, 'What like this?', and the guy
turns round – like a Red Indian – with this dart sticking in the
top of his head – and the girl is shrieking – but he doesn't
know what she's shrieking at – he can't feel anything! – and
my Dad looks up, and he takes in the scene in one, and he
shoos the hysterical female into the Ladies Changing Room
and then he says to the bloke: 'You just sit down there.
You've had a bit of an accident. Don't touch your head!' And
the ambulance came and under medical supervision the dart
was removed and the bloke was fine —
Well, actually he was subject to occasional winking fits.

And in George's caff you'll be likely to encounter Ken Kelly —
a gravel-voiced old-timer of the River —
Kelly is the only person who has an actual permit to LIVE on
   his boat —
and that's because his time on the Lea goes way back —
way back before the Marina and all that nonsense —
Ken Kelly can recall the BROTHEL BOATS OF THE LEA! —
and he'll recall them for you most mornings over breakfast.

There's a footbridge by George's which goes over to the Marina —
but we'll stay on the tow-path till we get to the quaint old white
   metal footbridge —

and we go over that and we're on Walthamstow Marsh —
to a pond —
and I'm having to cross this bridge and go to this pond every
    day —
because my little old mongrel dog has a commission.

— ❓ —

This is her commission:
she has to get all the over-night crap out of this particular
    pond —
(this pond was formed overnight by a doodle-bug, just like me,
    and maybe the same doodle-bug, date and geography offer it
    as a possibility) —
I don't throw sticks in for her —
she just plunges straight in and gets out any cans and crap —
(After that hurricane, wow, she was magnificent, she's only a
    slight little mongrel, but she found, in the water, she could
    move trees.)

— ❓ —

One morning, about thirty yards from the pond —
I could just see it through the grasses and coppice —
a picnic table of heavy wood, with heavy wood benches —
investigation —
the legs and supports are sunk deep into the ground —
definitely wasn't there yesterday —
and I don't like it —
it spoils the illusion I am 'Stalker' —
in the Zone.

— ❓ —

And days go by —
and every day I'm passing it —
and I never see anyone sitting at it —
and then one morning I sit at it —
and I think:
I know why it's been put here:
It's to be my Office.

— ❓ —

It was the first of that freak terrific weather —
(We've allowed all this pollution to invade the skies and the
    result is terrific weather —
a shame to waste it) —
and with the invention of the Cellnet telephone, do we need the
    walls and ceilings? —
? —
My Marsh Office —
this maybe qualifies as a Social Invention —
and I want to be interviewing people here —
I must get back into big cast theatre productions again —
I want all those actresses and people writing in with their c.v.s
    and photos —
and I'll send them the relevant pages of the London *A-Z*,
    marking George's caff as the place to report in —
and no-one to meet them —
they can have a cup of tea —
chance one of the cakes —
then in comes Ken Kelly —
Corncrake voice: 'Any thespians 'ere?' —
Kelly ushers you out and onto his old boat —
ships you off down river —
moors up under the Marsh bridge —
Captain Kelly looks about —
sniffs the air —

'Don't seem to want yer yet' —
Kelly scarpering the nine cats off the teapot —
some danger he's going to make you a cup of tea —
but from the office I let off a 506 Naval Distress Flare —
'Oo 'e's callin' for yer nah!' —
Ken Kelly pulls out a machete —
hacks a new path for you through the marsh grass —
then you get your first sight of me —
in my Marsh Office —
swinging deals on my Cellnet —
'Just sit down there—I'll be with you in a minute.'

— ❓ —

I'd get all this together and then it'd piss down —
but the answer is all along the banks of the Lea —
what I need is one of those enormous fisherman's umbrellas —
George says to go to Don's Fishing Tackle Emporium in
    Edmonton off the North Circular.

— ❓ —

Don's —
(Fishing tackle is mysterious and daunting) —
'Yes, sir?' —
Don presumably —
'I'm looking for one of those large fisherman's umbrellas
    please' —
'A 48 or a 51?' —
? —
'Erm – I'm not sure – you see I'm not a – it won't be for fishing –
    I've got an office on the Marsh – and I don't want my typing
    getting wet if it, er . . .' —

'Very healthy, the outdoors' says Don —
'Well is there a difference in price between the 48s and the
   51s?' —
'Yes sir – the 48s are cheaper because the 51s are bigger' —
I see a rack of them —
taking one out —
'What's this? Is this a 48?' —
'Yes, sir' —
'Can I see it up?' —
Enormous – it'd take up the whole width of the pavement —
48's ok for me —
then I find the extending prong attachment in the stem —
'the prong arrangement – is that any longer on the 51s?' —
'No, sir, the prong arrangement is uniform on all models' —
It's £28 —
I see an umbrella in the rack marked '£10' —
'Is this a 48?' —
'Yes, sir, but that's nylon' —
'Ah, nylon not as good as – this?' —
'Well, no, sir, in a mighty deluge you'll get a light mist under
   there' —
'O, well, no, that's no good for me, I'll have the first one' —
And then I find these marvellous fishing waistcoats —
WITH POCKETS ON THE POCKETS —
I'll have to have one of these —
just the job for a man with an office on the marsh —
(you can fit into the main pocket the *Complete Works* of Charles
   Fort) —
and I'm suddenly aware Don has a pretty young lady assistant
   and she's standing right by me, and she says: 'Have you really
   got an office on the Marsh?' —
'Oh, yes – got me little portable typewriter, me Cellnet –' —
PRETTY ASSISTANT: (CALLING OVER TO DON) 'You
   know your stuff gets used for all sorts of things – you know
   the big fishing-tackle boxes?' —
'Yes, I know, the BBC use them for make-up' —

'Yes, I know that, but as well the Women's Institute use them
    for competitive cake-making' —
(I don't feel I've ushered in one of Don's favourite days) —
ME: 'Anyway, I'd like one of these waistcoats' —
Don pointing at waistcoat: 'and 's not fer . . .' —
?—
'It's not for what?'
Don is pointing at a small square of fur on the top right of the
    coat —
'Snot Fur,' says Don, and mimes how, with your hands full of
    nets and rods, and it's a cold day, you can whisk away a dew-
    drop with your square of snot-fur.

— ? —

Next morning in the Office, getting the feel of the fisherman's
    waistcoat —
thrilling to the possibilities of the many pockets —
it would be possible, it seemed to me, to stiffen the pockets on
    the pockets with thin wood strips —
and make them into drawers —
A Chest of Drawers! —
Interviewing some actress, I'd pull out a drawer in the waistcoat,
    take out an index card, take down her particulars, pull out
    another drawer, and file her in an alphabetic system —
and a drawer for stamps and envelopes —
a built in calculator —
Pictures of Loved Ones —
But what on earth SHOW am I interviewing these folk for? —
I couldn't think of any show amazing enough to warrant these
    sensational interviewing techniques.

— ? —

But, sod it, let's just get on with the interviews —
Usually when you interview people, there you are, the Bollix,
   the Man with the Concept, and they have to prove and plead
   how they'll fit in —
these would be a new Marsh style of non-Fascistic interviews —
These techniques (grumpy Captain Kelly and his boat, the
   machete, the 506 distress flare, the Cellnet ringing constantly –
   I'd get a mate to keep ringing every three minutes during
   the interview – 'Well just try and keep it quiet and restrained,
   Donald, but I'll have to call you back, I'm seeing someone'—
   and not forgetting that the whole thing's taking place in the
   middle of a forgotten inner-urban wilderness!) would be likely
   to jolt the interviewee into the fabled 'awakened state' and
   he/she loose upon ME the Concept, or some strand of same.

— ❓ —

And as I came down from that moment of fine inspiration —
I felt I was not alone —
Prettyboy Tentringer is about to pronounce:
(It is my assumption that PBT and the Voice are one and the
   same) —
'Yes . . .' said Voice Prettyboy, and then 'Hmmm' —
'What?' I said —
Eventually I got it out of him —
That I shouldn't bring any of my old life and business to this
   Office —
'In this Office on the Marsh you should do MARSH
   BUSINESS' —
'What do you mean?'
But he was gone —
He left me with that.

— ❓ —

In this Office on the Marsh you should do Marsh Business.

— ? —

What is the Business of the Marsh?

— ? —

Be a Nature Poet?

— ? —

Keep a Marsh Diary?

— ? —

I was confused —
In this Office on the Marsh you should do Marsh Business.

— ? —

I doubt if I would have ever got anything together regarding
    'marsh business' if it hadn't happened to be peculiarly cold
    one morning —
I was setting off for the doodle-bug pond so the dog could
    perform her commission, but the cold was biting into the
    brain and I had to return for my hat —
but I couldn't find my hat —
but then I found A hat —
a dirty, knitted woolly hat, with a pom-pom on it —
(I couldn't recall ever having entertained the wearer of this hat) —

but I stuck it on and took the dog off to the pond —
When I got back, hat still on, I saw myself in the mirror —
'God', I thought, 'I can't go out like this —
I look like a Smurf!' —
but something kept me staring at this image of myself in the
    mirror —
the hat had a crudely knitted emblem on its front, which seemed
    to be a dolphin in a Christmas party hat behaving
    pornographically with a banana —
and the longer I looked at myself in this hat —
the more confirmed of opinion I became —
that the Man Who Does Marsh Business on the Marsh —
HE WEARS THIS HAT!

— ❓ —

You've heard of a 'thinking-cap'? —
I think there may be literal truth in it —
many, who habitually wear a hat, confirm this:
take your hat off for a few minutes in a pub or somewhere and
    sombody will be putting it on —
and when they do so, nine times out of ten —
THEIR BEHAVIOUR WILL BE MODIFIED FOR THE
    BETTER! —
As I understand it, when you think, a measurable amount of
    electrical energy is produced —
is it not likely that some would lodge in hat-grease?

— ❓ —

I kept the hat on —
I slept in it —
and it started taking me places —
it found for me a quaint, back-street shop which specialized in
    very old bicycles —

and it had me buy a very old lady's bike —
it took me to the Church Book Boutique, which only opens on
   Wednesday afternoons if the vicar feels like it, and we bought
   Sex Life of the Flowers and J. G. Ballard's *The Day of
   Creation* —
but when it had me buy twelve Chinese black and red note-
   books I got the picture —
I was to be the PASSIVE PROTAGONIST —
In my Marsh Office I would detail the days as they fell in my
   Marsh Journal —
sometimes I would be entering people's lives —
but subtly, peripherally, not enough to change them —
just enough to write about them —
the Guy Who is Around —
The Passive Protagonist —
The Man Who Does Marsh Business on the Marsh.

— ❓ —

And came the appointed morning and I rose early and Chinese
   notebook (now *Marsh Journal*, Vol I), *Sex Life of Flowers*
   and Ballard's *Day of Creation* all easily contained in
   fisherman's waistcoat pockets —
and I decided to take the 48 (even though it looked not at all
   like rain) and I fully extended the prong and set off on the old
   bike —
feeling terrific, like a Knight of Olde —
(but I had to go the long way round as I could only steer to the
   left) —
and I settled myself in at the Office —
Marsh Business —
The Passive Protagonist —
What was going to happen? —
Today and everyday? —
In my hat.

— ❓ —

And I began the *Marsh Journal* and I wrote:
'THE OFFICE. 7.23 a.m. – It may be the first day of Spring –
  Man with two dogs carrying stick goes by – Birds twittering –
  Pigeon fluttering and briefly soaring –' —
and it was a fine morning and the sun was streaming past my
  face and I was noticing that my eyebrows have now
  overgrown so unruly that it's like I'm looking through a hedge
  at everything —
and I try an experiment —
I take out a couple of clothes pegs —
(many years ago I discovered clothes pegs to be a superior paper
  clip) —
and I pegged up my brows —
terrific! —
I don't need glasses, just pegs! —
(It's commercially inadvisable for me to trim my eyebrows as I
  sometimes pick up these little parts on the telly playing
  somebody who's just invented something) —
'Dog asleep, or dozing rather, in the dewy grass clumps – Bike
  leant against table' —
And then I could write no more —
because out of the bushes behind the pond, had appeared a
  young man whose body language was so alarming it would not
  have by-passed the eye-muscles of an idiot.

— ? —

And he had with him a plastic bag —
with some weight of substance at the bottom of it —
and he plunged his head into the bag and took an obscenely
  deep breath from it —
and then commenced kicking shit out of invisible people —
'Fuck! and Fuck! and Fuck Off! and Fuck!' —

and then he saw me —
and he paused —
and then he roared: 'Clothes PEGS!!!' —
and he delivered the word 'pegs' in THE SHOUT:
THE LEGENDARY NOISE WHICH KILLS RATS AT A
     HUNDRED YARDS.

— ❓ —

And I had heard [and suffered from] that noise before —
1970 when I had my touring comedy troupe, 'Ken Campbell's
     Roadshow' —
and we were honoured —
I was asked to address the Symposium of World Theatre —
all the theatre-producing nations of the world had sent two
     delegates to London's Old Vic —
except for the Philippine Islands who'd sent thirty-seven —
and I was on a panel with Max Stafford-Clark, still the Artistic
     Director of the Royal Court Theatre, Sloane Square, but then
     heading the Traverse's touring wing, and the bloke from the
     Welfare State Troupe —
the young hopefuls of British Theatre —
and hungry for World Tours we told the world about
     ourselves —
I think I may have over-intellectualized what we were about but
     I sought to repair that in my concluding statement: '. . . but
     often we just race into the venues like lunatics and take it
     from there' —
and we'd all said our say, and the Chairman asked the World if
     it had any questions —
and from its ranks rose this maniac Brit —
'Yes,' he said, 'I've got a question for Mr Campbell —
you say you race into your venues like lunatics —
why don't you race in like DIABETICS —
and vomit over your audience?' —

and when he hit that syllable 'bet of 'diaBETics' —
that's when he hit the RAT-KILLING TIMBRE —
and he got me in the knee with it —
and I rose to reply but my knee had no 'spannung' to it and I fell
    under the table —
this excited the maniac to further excess —
some World Delegates, nervous of terrorism, now leaving —
Maniac now coming up to the platform —
desperately trying to hold my knee together in a half hobble,
    half hop —
I flee the stage —
followed by Welfare State chap, Chairman —
Max Stafford-Clark, bravely, I thought at that moment, the last
    to leave, even attempting dialogue with the Maniac —
but then giving it up, and now joining us, and Max kind enough
    to escort me to the bar and buy me a large Scotch —
and then Max says:
'I'm sorry about my Father' —
and my voice came out and it was like a little boy's voice and it
    said:
'Was that your Dad? —
I didn't bring my Dad.'

— ❓ —

And now, once more, on the Marsh, that mythic bellow, and it's
    got me in the knee again —
and I rise and fall —
and gathering the books together, and my 48 —
and lurker now coming towards me —
waving bag of substance —
gait of Ancient Messenger on last legs —
and me holding knee and hopping round to bike —
and 'I'm only BREATHING' he says —
'just TRAINING' and he slaps himself ludicrously hard on the

chest, and crouches briefly presumably to persuade me he's
into ski-jump practice on the Marsh —
and he's got two teeth missing at the front —
and there's slobber on his chin —
and a pus-encrusted wart on his nose —
and stuck in it what looked like a snapped off cocktail stick.

— ❓ —

And I'm on the bike, with all impedimenta, wobbling off toward
the river, dog following —
I fall off —
'You all right?' he calls —
'Yes, fine' – I wave him away —
and wheel the bike and stuff far out of range.

— ❓ —

A little sit —
a little rest by the river —
and then I get up and I'm testing my joints and they're not too
bad —
and I had my 48 on my back, and I catch sight of my shadow —
and something about it brings to mind the Seven Samurai —
and I hear the Samurai music —
and I resolve to return —
we shall return.

— ❓ —

Back at the Office —
I decide not to write any more —
the Breather is in the bushes bag in hand —

I pose as a bloke reading Ballard's *Day of Creation* —
I say 'pose', I was just taking the sort of time it would take to
 get to the end of a page and turn it, and I am aware that the
 Breather is now standing over me —
'Is that your book?' he says —
'Yes' I say —
'Would like to see where it writes about me?' he says —
he takes the book as one who knows it well —
(he has put his bag of strange substance on the Office table) —
he is dribbling —
he shows me a name in the book:
'Chad' —
'Is that your name – "Chad"?' —
'Yeah' —
This is the sentence:
'Why not go to the Sudan, or Chad?' —
Chad became my first regular client in the Office.

I have seen into Chad's bag —
fumey, green-tinged putty —
in coils like an old brain —
One morning he tells me of his ambition:
to be a pop star —
but he had a dis-quiet about following his dream —
'Why do all singers go gay?' —
'I don't know,' said the Passive Protagonist, 'it is odd now you
 mention it – why do all singers go gay?' —
Well, if he was going to be a singer HE WASN'T GOING TO
 GO GAY! —
This lemming instinct of all singers to plunge themselves into the
 abyss of gaydom, frankly sickened him —
The Passive Protagonist encouraged him to give it a shot, hoping
 that the world would be ready for such a revolutionary
 approach —

'I mean trees aren't gay,' he said, 'you don't get gay trees –' —
The Passive P was tested here; now well into *The Sex Life of
    Flowers* he could have argued the point, but 'No,' he said,
    'trees aren't gay –' —
'Or ants –' —
he was peering down at some ants —
he thought long and dribbled a bit, then he said: 'Actually
    there's no telling with ants –' —
and it was a fine morning and he took a huge belt from his
    bag —
and the sun was streaming through his hair —
(and his teeth) —
and I sensed he had a vision coming on —
I gave him space to have it —
It came: 'It's like this, isn't it,' he said, 'it goes in here' (pointing
    at the mouth) 'as food . . . and then . . .' (long pause) 'it
    turds out –' —
'Hmmm –' I said, then: 'Wow!' —
'But what does it get up to while it's in you? YOU DON'T
    KNOW – I don't know and you don't know —
food could act in gay ways in your body, it could be acting in a
    gay way NOW AND YOU WOULDN'T KNOW IT —
Christ!' he said —
(bleakly, he put his head in his bag, and then emerging:) —
'A thought like that could obsess you to study up and become
    the greatest surgeon the world has ever known – and you'd
    cut yourself open to catch your food acting in gay ways but as
    soon as it saw you were looking – IT'D STOP DOING IT
    AND YOU'D NEVER KNOW!.

— ❓ —

In lighter vein: 'Can you tickle yourself?' asked Chad —
'I don't think it's possible,' I said —
'For a successful bout of tickling the "to be tickled person" (or

"prospective ticklee") must not be able to predict the
   precise spots which are to be tickled' —
'Yeah?' he said —
and he put his head in his bag, and the instant he emerged he
   commenced tickling himself and cackling hysterically —
I was impressed.

— ? —

It occurred to me that a semi-feral chap like Chad might have
   bizarre powers —
'Can you do things, Chad?' I asked —
'Like what?' he said, dubiously —
'I don't know,' I said, 'like make yourself invisible, make things
   appear, that sort of thing. . . ?' —
He looked at me a long time —
he disappeared his whole head into the bag —
this time it seemed he was not merely indulging in the fumes —
but looking directly into the old green brain for an answer —
when he came out he seemed to be remembering . . . something
   . . . he scrabbled up a stone and he put it on the Office
   table —
'I can move things,' he said, 'I could move that stone from there
   to there –' (indicating a distance of approximately four
   inches) —
'What, with the power of your mind?' —
'Yeah,' he said —
'Could you do it now?' —
He sat down at the table —
he focussed his powers on the stone —
minutes —
he sought further inspiration from the bag —
and then he remembered something else —
'Yeah!' he said, 'yeah – I could move it – I COULD! – but if I
   did, the smell it would make would be APPALLING!'

— ? —

In the Office, evening approaching —
and suddenly, Chad —
and he says: 'Have you ever been in a filter bed?' —
'No?' I said —
'Are you up to it?' he says —
'OK' – having no idea what this adventure might entail.

— ❓ —

And it's on, Chad leading, further south down the tow-path of
   the Lea —
under the railway viaduct, under the last two arches of which, in
   the early 1900s Alliott Verdon Roe (Avro) had his
   workshops, and but a few weeks after Kitty Hawk had his
   motorbike engined tri-plane rising nine foot off the ground,
   thus pioneering Britain's first powered manned flight over
   Walthamstow Marshes —
and then, Avro and butler-cum-mechanic into the riverside
   tavern, the Anchor and Hope, there to spend the night telling
   the tale —
The Anchor and Hope, where to this day, the stranger is
   greeted with bright eyes —
regulars vie to have you, and not to turn you over, not
   usually —
have no fear of those unshaven faces —
something there —
the slow flowing water of the Lea? —
contemplation of the Marshes across? —
local deity? —
is it built on a conjunction of ley-lines? —
or is it Avro's return which is subconsciously awaited? —
but something keeps always, whatever the weather, several
   drinkers outside, and making of them all, philosophers —

but drink not being his poison, Chad leads on, ignoring the
  importunes of the philosophers, to stay, at least for one pint
  of Les's excellently kept Fuller's —
And under the Lea Bridge (of the Lea Bridge Road) —
crossing now the Lea by the bridge by the weir —
river, rubbish and rats to the right —
high Victorian brick wall to the left, wrought iron gates, more
  wall —
and then round the back —
now on Hackney Marshes, drained, tamed and turned into a
  hundred football pitches by soldiers of the British Army, a
  therapy to debrief and un-excite them, following their victory
  over Jap and German —
a measure to reduce silliness on demob —
and then, Chad and I, breaking in through concrete fencing —
and we're now in the Abandoned Filter Beds —
and let me tell you what these things are:
THEY ARE ENORMOUS SWIMMING BATHS FULL OF
  VEGETATION AND FOLIAGE!

— ? —

I said: 'Chad! How did you know to bring me here?!' —
But he was swinging from trees and gibbering —
he had the gift of tongues now —
he was in the grip of Eospeech.

— ? —

There are six enormous swimming baths —
usually —
sometimes there are seven —
and they were engineered in the 1840s —

London was drinking loads of Lea water and cholera hit big —
and these enormous swimbath things were a system of filtering
   the water —
and they'd been used up till twenty years ago —
and then abandoned —
And Nature had been allowed her reign —
and in one bath she'd ordered a bulrush and reed bed —
in another, high surging marsh grasses surrounding a green
   limpopo lagoon —
another is the sea-side —
but the one down into which I was often to return, is an
   entanglement of luminous green sapling growth and vine —
and down there —
I found it —
(about twenty feet from the wall) —
THE SITE OF THAT DREAM.

— ❓ —

And one time, down there, this thought came:
That dream was long ago —
at the time of that dream this was all under water.

— ❓ —

The Big Case:
The Passive Protagonist is in the Office —
Over the white metal footbridge she comes —
short red skirt —
white top, lacey and laundered —
red high heels —
the very long black hair —
She was originally from Taiwan and her name should've been
   something of a warning:
EMMA MAY WANG.

— ❓ —

The first thing she said: 'I was told I'd find you here in your hat.'

— ? —

The case:
That since 1984 Miss Wang has been writing —
a novel about nurses and songs —
only to find her stuff coming out on the radio, the next day after
   composition —
Is, she wants to know, her phone being bugged? —
'If your phone is being bugged,' I tell her, 'it's as well to know
   this: bugging will make of your receiver, a listening ear at
   ALL times, not just when you're on the phone' —
'Can they read thoughts?' she asked —
'No,' I said, 'I don't think there's a bug invented that can read
   thoughts . . . there might be one which can monitor
   brainwaves but I think all you'd get from that is wavy lines on
   graph paper' —
I hardly think you could deduce a novel about nurses from
   them —
I said it was likely this: that she'd been working hard on a song,
   honing down some line of lyric, and then hears something
   similar on the radio, and thinks: 'Hey! that's mine!' —
She said, No, she didn't think it was that.

— ? —

'Well, maybe you're precognitive, Miss Wang,' I said —
'Maybe you are actually predicting what'll be on tomorrow's
   radio' —
No, she didn't think it was that —
She wondered if it might have something to do with that when

she was made redundant as a nurse, and decided to write
this novel about nursing, that she'd discussed her intention
with a certain Detective Inspector of Longton.

— ❓ —

'Well,' I said, and 'Wow —
and what's this certain Detective Inspector so worried that
    you're going to write? —
so worried that he puts a bug on your phone, night and day, for
    years!? —
What's your picture of this constabulary in Longton? —
shifts of trainee policemen monitoring your bug? —
"Oy!" (guy in headphones) "shut up everyone – she's
    humming!" —
and they crowd round the headset, all these coppers, and they
    get the hang of your latest song —
and sirens blaring they race round to the recording studio —
three hours later it's on wax and *neee-naww! neee-naww!* to the
    local radio station —
and they've got some sinister hold over the Dee-Jay we
    suppose —
"Have this on the air tomorrow, or else, Chum!" —
Ludicrous —
Isn't Longton in the Potteries?' —
Yes, that's right, she lives in Stoke-on-Trent, but this has been
    going on for years and all her friends tell her to give up
    writing, 'cos obviously it's no use if the stuff is going out on
    the radio the next morning —
But I'm not sure, Miss Wang, with your long black hair, that
    your friends have given you the best advice —
put aside your novel, put aside your songs for a bit —
what you're talking to me here and now about —
that is a SUBJECT! —
If you're fantasizing all this, it is still of interest —

if you are precognitive it is very much of interest —
and if anything's going on like you think is going on, just calmly
   assemble the facts, and YOU COULD BE SITTING ON A
   GOLD-MINE.

— ❓ —

She lived in Stoke-on-Trent, but came to London every ten days
   or so —
and she'd come and see me in the Office —
Half of *Marsh Journal*, Vol II, is devoted to our weird
   conversations —
but I choose not to entertain you with them —
(Just this —
she said one time: 'I bought a guinea pig to love . . . but all it
   did was shit and hide') —
Ah.

— ❓ —

But she loved those cakes —
George's post-war, noodles of coconut cakes —
she'd eat three at a sitting —
and it was outside George's caff, that she asked: 'Have you got a
   Black and Decker drill?' —
'Yes –' —
With a half inch diameter drill bit?' —
'Possibly –?' —
Could she borrow them? —
What for? —
She had problems . . . with her shelving – what would really be
   best is if I could go back with her to her home in Stoke-on-
   Trent and help her with her shelving –? —
I told her that, no, that wouldn't be possible, and although I put

in all the time I could in the Office, that I was actually very
busy, that I was, myself, in the middle of a script, in fact in
the middle of two, and so the idea of taking time out to go off
with her to Stoke-on-Trent had to be out —
Reluctantly, no, not possible —
And then I heard myself saying: 'Except, maybe, for a couple of
days . . .'

A small frog fell from the sky —
(dropped from the bill of a high-flying goose, I reason) —
landing stunned, on the ground, by our feet —
and I promptly picked up the little creature and threw it in the
    Lea —
I think I regretted the action.

I got off the train at Stoke —
my little bag of tools —
the heavy gloss black hair was on the platform, its weight
    unruffled by the wind —
into a taxi —
It became clear that she thought there were two of us —
that some of the times on the Marsh, she had been interviewed
    by maybe my brother, (I have none), or cousin —
She saw lampposts as sexually depraved Authority figures.*

*'I tell of a woman, who by mental picturings, not only marked the body of her
unborn infant, but transformed herself into the appearance of a tiger, or a
lamppost, or became a weretiger, or a werelamppost—'
                                            Charles Fort, *Wild Talents*.

The layout and furnishings of her small terraced house, were
   very similar to those of my parents' old semi-bungalow in
   Ilford —
Emma informed me that during her last visit to London she'd
   suffered a break-in —
apparently the local constabulary, in league with the BBC and
   certain people from Channel 4, had broken in, and inserted
   fast-breeding phosphorus machines into the ceilings, and that
   there was now a rain of invisible, but deadly particles.

— ❓ —

She prepared a meal – vegetables in curious batter, and
   shrimps, – under a parasol —
and to outwit the BBC and Co., we ate it UNDER THE
   TABLE —
and she described how, when alone, she pecked at her meals out
   of a drawer —
then she said: 'If your eyes come out, can they be put back?' —
I said that, no, they couldn't —
She said: 'I thought they could –' —
I said: 'Well, no, they can't' —
She got out from under the table; she left the room; and she
   came back with a Phrenology Head —
and she asked me to find for her, on her own head, her Area of
   Hope —
and I found it for her, tapping on the spot on her skull, relishing
   the excuse to feel her hair —
'People's heads don't ever just fall off, do they. . . ?' she said —
I told her they didn't —
and she sought my opinion on St Phyllis, evidently a Catholic
   Martyr, who, upon decapitation, had picked up her head and
   kissed it —
and I said: 'Could we get on with the shelves now?'

— ❓ —

But not quite yet, apparently —
something that could only be done by one needed preparing
    first —
the shelving problem was in her upstairs —
and she took my tool bag —
I was bade stay down in the dining parlour —·
I was looking around to see how I might pass my time till I was
    summoned —
'Hey!' I called up to her, 'Where's your radio? and TV?' —
She had thrown them out because —
THEY HAD STARTED TO ADDRESS HER DIRECTLY.

— ? —

I sat for a short while —
I began to see specks in the air —
but these were presumably not phosphorus particles, as those, I
    had been informed, were invisible —
and then I began to poke about through her things.

— ? —

And one drawer was full of feathers —
and in another drawer I found large format photos of beaches —
(some were maybe deserts) —
and on many of the photos was writing —
in silver ink —
I guess lines from her lyrics —
'Oh, when's the time for coming home?' —
and 'The years fly by like fruit gums' —
and 'In May I wear my Orange Coat' —
and I was now hearing the buzz of the drill from upstairs —

I supposed I ought to go up and help —
but I'd just seen, in a corner, what looked like a two-foot high
   wooden feather —
I investigated, and, no, not a feather, an erotic statuette, turned
   modestly to the wall:
a red man, crouching in green trousers, and reaching up,
   literally, into the nethers of a long black-haired goddess, left
   knee raised high —
and the drilling had stopped —
and then I saw that Emma May Wang was at the foot of the
   stairs —
and she was smiling, uncharacteristically, beautifully,
   CHIRPILY —
LIKE A YOUNG GIRL, WHO'S JUST SCORED A GOAL
   AT A HOCKEY MATCH.

And then I was conscious of a strange smell —
what's that smell? —
and then I realized —
Oh yes! —
(oh blimey) —
I WAS EXUDING THE STICKY OF CHILDHOOD.

And love is now being made —
foot of the stairs, standing position —
and, black hair of the goddess —
this is probably the sublimest moment, so far, of your tacky life,
   Campbell —
but might it not even be topped? —
if we could shift the proceedings onto the sofa over there? —

that sofa, so like my old Mum and Dad's . . .
and then I was aware that I was looking at blood.

— ❓ —

And coming out of the blood was wire —
a round hole of pulsing blood in her head —
she'd trepanned herself with the Black and Decker —
made a hole in her Hope —
(been fixing her own shelving) —
But what to make of the wire . . .
I said: 'You just sit down there – You've had a bit of an
    accident – Don't touch your head –' —
looking up the directory for the hospital number —
(What is that wire. . . ? —
Like some awful AERIAL —
Has she been so missing her radio that she's making an
    experiment in Direct Reception. . . ? —
Looking at the wire made my teeth go funny) —
Through to the hospital —
They're only sending out ambulances on emergencies —
I said: 'Well this is a lady who's just bored a hole in her
    head –' —
'Can she walk?' —
I said, 'I dunno –' —
'Well, see if she can walk –' —
(the hospital was just up the hill, she said) —
I tried a taxi firm but they'd got no taxis —
well, let's see if she can walk . . .
yes, she's fine, she's happy to walk —
and I tidied her up —
and holding her gently but firmly —
(I didn't want to spill her) —
we set off into the night.

— ❓ —

And it was one of those nights when you hear a lot of wind, but
    you don't feel any —
and as we rounded the corner, and only up the hill to go —
my shoes —
I had these heavy black shoes on —
and I was worried, holding her tight and steady, that the click of
    the heels might jolt her —
so I took them off and put them over a hedge into someone's
    garden —
and as we passed the church, I was surprised, given the lateness
    of the hour, to hear a congregation lustily singing a hymn —
but then the hymn STUCK —
and restarted a few phrases back —
and I thought: That's no congregation in there —
it's a lonely vicar playing his records —
and I give that as the moment that I realized I had fallen in love
    with Emma May Wang —
and I was OK about the aerial —
and it wasn't an aerial, it was a feather —
its plumes and barbs blown on the wind.

— ❷ —

Through the imposing gates of the Infirmary —
up an avenue of trees —
my arm around her —
a couple of some style —
Doors, more like those of a fine old hotel, are opened for us —
and a red carpet! —
and of a rich pile, I can attest, through my socks.

— ❷ —

And she is seen commendably quickly —
and she'd said no word from the bottom of her stairs till now —
but now, with the handsome young doctor, she is speaking
    lucidly:
You see, she'd had this feeling, this thought, well not a thought,
    more a feeling, that she hadn't got any brain, and it had kept
    bothering her, this doubt, so she'd thought well let's get this
    worry out of the way, and so she'd bored the hole in her head,
    and felt in with coat-hanger wire, and she was so pleased to
    find that, yes, there was a load of stuff in there, and so happy
    that she was now with someone who knew what he was doing
    who could get it out for her, because you never knew the sort
    of damage you might do, playing about like this, did you.

— ☉ —

Three weeks later I was talking to a Medical Philosopher outside
    the Anchor and Hope —
he knew Emma a bit —
'Where exactly did she do it?' —
'Right here,' I said, indicating my Area of Hope —
'Wow!' he said, 'well, she got it right – not so many years ago,
    when they used to do that operation a lot, actually they got a
    lot of success with it – she could have done herself a favour
    there, her – the mistake was the coat-hanger wire.'

— ☉ —

I had to stay more than the 'couple of days' in Stoke —
and in the crematorium chapel —
three neighbours, and Gent in Raincoat —
(the certain Detective Inspector from Longton?) —
organ —
and then Frank Bailey, nice man, the Funeral Director, beside
    me —

and he passes me a plastic bag —
and in it —
I'd asked Frank if I could be allowed a lock of Emma's hair —
here, in the bag, was the entire mane —
and the organ swells —
jubilantly —
doors open themselves —
we see the gas jets —
and the coffin is conveyed by a roller system towards the
     flames —
the doors tastefully closing themselves before its journey's end.

And no-one to stop me and I took the statuette —
and on the train back to London, the Black and Decker in my
     tool-bag with the hair, and the erotic statuette —
and my hands reached into the bag and they felt the hair —
and they brought out the statuette —
and it didn't seem at all the thing to be seen with on a British
     train, so I kept it under the table —
but handling the rampant totem, I may have come close to
     comprehending what had REALLY taken me to Stoke —
something like this?:
that I had been seeking my redemption through a Red Indian
     Phantasm Lady —
but as to whether, by her brief and curious incarnation I had
     gained it —
that was severely open to doubt.

THREE

And back home now —
and outside George's caff —
and eating (deliberately) a post-war noodle cake —
staring into the oily murk of the Lea —
thoughts and memories (and regrets) —
slow-flowing —
merging —
and off to the pub —
Opening Time to well past Drink Up, with the Philosophers,
    outside the Anchor and Hope, chummy, huddled, in an early
    snow-fall —
and on the stagger home, passing the riverside flats of
    Watermint Quay, in the lock-up for the residents' dustbins,
    the lock broken, and intending to winter in there:
CHAD.

— ❷ —

But Chad now, sadly, mutated into his own Mother —
wrapped in a lady's coat which was on the turn from green to
    brown —
(or vice-versa) —
and saying over: 'Oh look at his shoes! Will you look at my
    boy's shoes! The state of them!' —
and, indeed, there wasn't much left of his shoes —

and I said: 'Don't worry about your shoes, Chad – I'll sort your
   shoes out – just hang on here –' —
and I nipped off home —
my intention to bring him a tenner —
he could go to the Spastics shop in the morning, and get himself
   shod for ten quid —
(probably have a bit over for a jersey) —
but I found myself going back with £200 —
Chad muttering into his plastic bag —
I showed Chad the notes —
made him aware of the enormous amount —
and as I gave him the money I took from him his plastic bag of
   substance —
'But that's for this,' I said, 'and I don't mean just this bag – for
   ever – no more bags – do you understand?' —
and I think he did —
he felt around in one of the bins and produced a miniature oil
   painting —
flowers in a blue vase —
and he gave it to me —
and then, before his gaze, I threw his bag of substance into the
   Lea.

— ● —

And I went home, and couldn't reason with why I didn't feel
   better about the transaction —
I'd given him 200 quid —
I'd taken his substance from him —
(I'd taken his substance from him) —
I'D TAKEN HIS SUBSTANCE FROM HIM! —
O shit! —
That suddenly had a dark ring —
I ran back down to the bins —
He wasn't there —

I spent the whole of the next day in the Office —
He didn't show up —
Or the next day —
I never saw him again —
(except I fear I may.)

— ❓ —

Outside George's caff —
Captain Ken Kelly eating an egg, and dredging up memories of
    Dotty the water-tart —
and suddenly I said: 'There's a body going by!' —
George came out, and we looked in the river —
and it might be a body —
if it was floating by arse up —
we watched the thing pass slowly under the bridge —
perhaps it wasn't a body —
and back to Dotty and the Brothel Boat Era when everything
    round here was fucking terrific.

— ❓ —

But a couple of days later George said to me:
'You were right – it was a body – they fished it out at Old Ford
    Lock –' —
I said: 'What happens to a body after it's fished out at Old Ford
    Lock?' —
George said: 'It'd go to Hackney Mortuary.'

— ❓ —

'How well did you know your missing person?' said the man at
    Hackney Mortuary —

I said I'd met him on several occasions —
'So you didn't know him well enough to make a positive
    identification with the body alone?' —
(What does he mean? —
He's going to come with me and pull out the drawer, isn't
    he?) —
What he meant was without the head —
I said: 'What's happened to the head?' —
He said: 'It's gone to Farringdon –' —
I said: 'Why?' —
He said: 'It happens. I'll give you the address if you like.'

— ? —

Farringdon —
N. Evans Associates and I was in luck —
they were closed —
perhaps they were taking an early lunch —
maybe they get all the heads sorted by Wednesday —
Anyway, I thought, sod it, had enough, going home.

— ? —

Platform Farringdon Tube Station deserted —
then enter two roaring men —
lurching, rolling and both called Jimmy —
I took up a bizarrely unalarming posture by the chocolate
    machine —
I by-passed the musculature of Jimmy One's eyeballs, but failed
    with Jimmy Two's —
I turned slowly from the chocolate machine and was faced with
    SEETHE —
a squat, hideous man built like half a dozen shit-houses —
WRATH —

So filled with wrath he couldn't speak —
coming from his mouth and nose a disgusting foam —
but then, through the nauseous froth, came words, and they
    were these:
'I'M GOING TO THROW YOU ON THE LINES!' —
I said, 'Why?'
He said: 'YOU KNOW WHY!!' —
I said: 'Well, I'm sorry, I don't –' —
Froth, foam, then:
'BECAUSE I'M POTTY AND I'M GOING TO DRIVE YOU
    POTTY AND THEN I'M GOING TO THROW YOU ON
    THE LINES!' —
The train comes in —
I dodge him —
I'm on the tube —
but so is he —
in pursuit —
Tube starting off —
and he's pursuing me up the carriage —
I have to go through the emergency door into the next
    carriage —
he's through it too —
falling on people, roaring, but keeping up —
and King's Cross and I'm out and escaped.

But I hadn't escaped damage from the encounter —
it was my neck —
I'd lost the lubrication of the neck vertebrae —
or maybe it was psychological —
and that I was scrunching down my head —
so as to be sure it was still there.

— ? —

Whichever the cause, it was a depressing state —
and come the Saturday I knew I must take the cheering up of
   myself in hand —
I decided to go to Dingwall's Market at Camden Lock —
(memories of great times in that place) —
but I wasn't prepared for how popular it's become —
and the noise and the throng and my neck —
it was too much effort to fight through to a favourite stall:
The Stall of Wooden Ties —
they look like regular ties —
could be mistaken for suede —
hand-carved by P.C. Slade, the whittling constable of Crediton,
   Devon —
but, as I say, I'd passed it by —
but the carving copper caught up with me —
he showed me his new line:
'With Designer Woodworm' —
and he put his latest model on me —
(a ribbon Velcros round the neck) —
and he wanted no money for it —
he'd seen me in something on the telly and assumed I now
   mixed with important people —
'You'll wear it?' he said —
'Yes,' I said —
he battled back to his stall —
and wood tie around my creaky neck —
I felt like a fully paid up member of the Dick Society.

I'd now got round to the back of the market —
behind the Le Routier Restaurant (pricey but good) —
and was resting amongst the splendid absence of happy people
   by the canal lock —
could just see the last market stall through the trellis —

an Objet de Crap stall —
and then I was aware that I was not alone —
a man probably in his mid-twenties —
good-looking in a way —
a cut down white shirt and tight black trousers —
the sort of job you'd play Hamlet in —
and he said: 'Have you ever been in love?' —
I said: '. . . Yes –' —
and he said: 'Have you ever fallen in love suddenly, with such
    an intensity, that you knew you had to possess that
    person?' —
I said: '. . . Something like that . . . possibly . . . yes –' —
He said: 'I'm Noddy –' —
and he held out a large hand —
and I gave him mine —
and squeezing it into pain, smiling, he said: 'What's your
    name?' —
'Ken –' —
He said: 'Why aren't you talking to me, Kenneth?' DID YOU
    THINK YOU'D FOUND A SAFE PLACE AT LAST?' —
I said: 'Why did you squeeze my hand so hard?' —
He said: 'Because I wanted you to feel my skin; my flesh – I
    would like you to feel my heart –' —
and he took my hand and put it inside his shirt —
and he said: 'It's pumping very hard, isn't it; very fast. . . ?' —
'Yes it is –' —
'But it's not love though – that's the unfortunate part, Kenneth –
    it's hate – the real thing – Here's how it'll go:
we'll just hang around here until whatever it is wells up inside
    me and whatever has to be done will do itself —
I am merely to be the agency.'

— ② —

I have done a course on How to be a More Remarkable
    Person —

and one of the tips we got was:
If you encounter a dangerous customer you should note which is
    the weaker side of the face, and you should look, without
    deviation, into the eye of the weaker side —
and this, I had been doing for some time, with Noddy.

— ❓ —

But, looking intently at one point, one still retains a
    considerable peripheral vision —
and I had been hoping to see a friend turn up in it —
and then just anybody —
but so far no-one —
I was aware only of what I'd taken to be a cloth mushroom,
    which I could see through the trellis, hanging from the awning
    of the Objet de Crap stall —
and at this moment it was caught in the breeze and it turned
    round and I saw that it wasn't a cloth mushroom, it was a doll,
    a little oriental doll lady, and I thought:
so this is my only Area of Hope —
that Miss Emma May Wang is right now interceding for me on
    some other plane —
and Noddy is saying: 'You put people into compartments don't
    you?' —
and I said: '. . . Sometimes –' —
'Which of your compartments are you putting me in?' —
I said: 'I don't have one ready for you yet –' —
and he said: 'Are you acquainted with the music of Wagner?' —
and suddenly my head was a riot in a telephone exchange but
    from somewhere way at the back of the mayhem was someone
    jumping, shouting, determined that through the confusion his
    message would get through, and it was Prettyboy Tentringer
    and he was shouting and he was shouting and I couldn't hear
    through the noise of the Pandemonium and then I heard and
    then I heard and what he was saying was:

'SPEAR HIM!' —
and I ripped off my tie and speared the awful fellow into the
   canal.

— ❓ —

And when I got home I thought: 'I think I better get out of
   London –' —
I know, go and visit my friends in Liverpool —
I pack a few things —
Euston Station —
in line for my ticket, and I think, no, I can't go to Liverpool
   because the train stops at STOKE-ON-TRENT —
and then I think, I know, I'll go to Paddington Station —
I couldn't think what all places you might go to from Paddington
   Station —
and I thought, well, if I don't know where I'm going nor will
   anyone else.

— ❓ —

And so now coming up from the Tube onto Paddington Station
   Main Line —
passing the statue of Isambard Kingdom Brunel, seated, and
   looking askance, it seems, at our latest engineering feat —
the nine-seater plastic pod arrangement —
so that nine people may sit on the same seat with minimum
   chance of meeting —
circular pods —
I sat on a pod to study the Menu of Possibilities —
and then happening to glance at the Taxi queue just past
   Platform 8 —
heading the queue was ANDY JONES! —
ANDEE! —

But by the time I got there he'd disappeared —
(into a taxi I suppose) —
but coming back from the rank I am passing between the cars
   parked slantwise towards the exit slip road and it seems to me
   that I am passing my old mauve Marina —
what was its registration? —
can't remember —
but I note the keys have been left in the ignition —
and I return to my pod —
and I read through the list of places served from Paddington —
I read through the list three times —
and I find it very depressing reading —
many places —
but really no place to go.

— ❓ —

'He went for an ice-cream at the interval' —
'He went around the horses' —
He went to Paddington Station —
what was this (vision?) of Andy Jones? —
to disappear? —
vanish? —
teleport off? —
and I fancied I knew how it might be accomplished —
comes into my mind the opening page of *LO!*:
'A naked man in a city street HYPHEN the track of a horse in
   volcanic mud HYPHEN the mystery of reindeer's ears
   HYPHEN' —
and the hyphens (—) were beginning to lift off the page —
'an appalling cherub appears in the sea HYPHEN' —
and now the hyphen is beginning to turn towards me —
and when it points directly at me —
that's when I'll go! —
'Showers of frogs and blizzards of snails' —

HYPHEN almost at me now —
and then the Voice is shrieking: 'Don't you think there are one
  or two items you should pay for before you leave?' —
I said: 'Lord, what do you mean? You mean there IS a Hell?' —
'Yes, it's for those who've ever thought there was one –' —
'And it's bad is it?' —
'It's as bad as you've ever thought it was –' —
I was thinking, up past your ears in bubbling shit and a duff
  snorkel —
'Don't be optimistic,' said the Voice.

And the Voice said: 'Would you like me to organize a
  punishment for you here?' —
I said: 'Like what?' —
and the Voice said: 'Well you know that car you saw with the
  key in the ignition? —
go and steal it –' —
I thought and I said No —
I said: 'No, I don't want to do that –' —
and the Voice said: 'That's how come it would have been a
  punishment –' —
I was beginning to get a handle on the concept —
and then the Voice came up with another suggestion: 'Take your
  little bag of belongings and go down into the Gentlemen's
  Convenience –' —
(I looked to see where this was – beyond Platform 1) —
'Go into whichever cubicle seems to summon you, put your bag
  on the lavatory seat, take off all your clothes, and pile them
  up on top of the bag, and set light to it all in three places —
AND THEN STEAL THE MARINA!' —
I said: 'And then I'll be happy?' —
The Voice said: 'I think there's a chance –' —
I said: 'Are you inside me or outside me?' —

and the Voice said: 'I'm not going to tell you –' —
And then the Voice said: 'I'll tell you if you do it.'

— ❷ —

And that's how come I'm going passed the Bureau de Change
    and the Croissant Shop, and turning right beside Platform 1,
    and towards the Gentlemen's Convenience, just by the Tie
    Rack —
and parked outside is an Electric Courtesy Vehicle, with driver,
    and passed them and down into the Gents —
and down there it is RED —
the ceilings are red —
the floor is red —
the cubicles are red —
and I'm now in one —
did it 'summon' me? —
I don't know —
maybe it did:
beside the WC pedestal is a pair of black shoes in good nick —
and they worry me, the shoes —
and I've taken all my clothes off —
they're in a pile, on my bag, on the lav seat —
but the shoes? —
are the shoes to be part of my pyrotechnic revel? —
No —
There was no mention of shoes —
they're innocent, bystander shoes —
and I set light to it all in three places —
deliberately firing the crutch of my trousers with the first
    match —
but I don't go —
and I don't know why —
it's gone from smouldering into burning —

and then my hand reaches through the flames and pulls from the
   bag —
EMMA'S HAIR.

— ❷ —

And with Emma's hair in my hand, I'm ok, and I'm out of the
   cubicle, and I'll tell you something peculiar about the
   Paddington Gents —
the cubicles are NUMBERED! —
I thought, what are they numbered for? —
Are we on TV? —
('Come out Number 9—your hour is up!—') —
and now passing a couple of guys having a piddle, and they
   don't see me, and up the stairs, and the Courtesy Vehicle is
   still there, but the driver has gone —
and then a middle-aged Hasidic gentleman —
I strike a bizarrely un-alarming pose —
AND HE DOESN'T SEE ME! —
and the folk at Menzie's haven't seen me —
and I'm now behind the Bureau de Change and the Croissant
   Shop —
at the Platform heads —
and creeping past a mother and daughter —
they don't see me because they're studying Arrival Times on a
   Video Monitor, Platform 2 —
But then —
coming down the alley to Platforms 3/4, two middle aged ladies,
   and a young man in ludicrously coloured shorts —
they have seen me —
and breaking into a run —
and a *Poop*! from behind me —
the Electric Courtesy Vehicle in pathetic pursuit —
(hey, my neck's ok!) —
but, now the alley which comes down to Platforms 5/6 —

Seen by a big, black British Rail Official —
and he's blowing his WHISTLE —
and seen by the Pod People —
and they're turning to each other —
My God, I've united the Pod People! —
(running flat out now) —
and the Taxi queue is EXCITED —
and coming down from the slip road a Royal Mail Van —
and the larger sort of postman getting out —
hue and cry! —
and it seems that everyone thinks that I'm making for the Taxi
    queue —
and I keep up this pretence —
and then when I get past Platform 8, I turn —
Now heading towards the Marina —
and I think I can make it —
AND THEN I PRAY —
(and let me tell you something about REAL prayer: it is
    LIQUID in form —
it comes squirting out of every pore) —
and this is my prayer:
'Let that not be my old Marina!' —
(that thing never started first time!) —
and I'm going to make it! —
and I'm in the car —
about to start it —
and then I remember that I've got a deal riding on this —
and I say: 'So are you INSIDE me or OUTSIDE me?' —
and the Voice says: 'You're inside ME.'

— ⊘ —

And I couldn't get the picture of that —
and that was my undoing —
car door flung open —

and I am flown from the car as if in a ballet —
and as I'm flown I'm able to see smoke gloriously issuing from
   the Gents on Platform 1 —
Fort said: 'An unclothed man shocks a crowd – a moment later,
   if nobody is generous with an overcoat, somebody is collecting
   handkerchiefs to knot around him –' —
that's how it was in the thirties —
(when the Brothel Fleet steamed the Lea) —
but things have changed —
they're quite violent now —
or maybe it was something about me? —
Emma's HAIR? —
they're hitting me into a mail-bag —
and the last thing I see is 'TRAVELLER'S REST' —
and then the RAMP which comes down onto the far end of the
   station.

— ❓ —

and then I was no longer on paddington station I was in
the swimming bath of veg and foliage at the appointed
spot and there was the geezer ten feet away and he had
his back to me and he was planting flowers and playing
golf and jerking off all in the same moment and I knew I
must get round there and meet him but I could only walk
in an agonizingly slow careful mince and I noted my
elbow was professionally bandaged perhaps I'd just had
an arsehole graft and now I've made it I've minced
round and I'm meeting the geezer and the large bulgy
eyes bring to mind andy jones but then the many arms
make me think of the prophet but most it's the frog from
the lino kissed into princehood and it's not he's speaking
it is that I am receiving from him and this is what I'm
receiving in my o-oringy coat in my o-oringy coat in my
o-oringy coat and was he wearing an orange coat no he

wasn't in my o-oringy coat constantly repeated and it was
doing something to me or undoing something in me in
my o-oringy coat as if all my life has been a wilful act of
forgetting in my o-oringy coat and I feel something
loosening in my o-oringy coat and suddenly whoop a trap
door at the back of my head has opened and another
trap door whoop at the front and I am hurtling
backwards and forwards through time at the same time
backwards past lives flying by like fruit gums I am now
way back I am something examining primordial ice an
onion and a lump of ice and what have they in common I
am looking at botanical forms in the first ice and I can
predict jungles and forwards I have gone so far forwards
yes these are machines and still in a sense enquiring on
but in a finitely cold system whose sun has died in my o-
oringy coat and turning round holding hand number
three of the many armed andy jones frog prophet miss
nscho-tchi wang all put back together and resplendently
adorned in a whole draw load of feathers in my o-oringy
coat and chad lurking in the luminous green young
sapling growth but no bag no bag no need of bag now in
my o-oringy coat in my o-oringy coat and they're trying
to get me to look at something the stones hey the stones
are shifting and moving and o wow and o wow non-
physical entities in a flash manifesting with sniggering
faces and exquisite wings in my o-oringy coat in my o-
oringy coat and then I see it yes I see it the thread of
marching time and I see the actual thread in my o-oringy
coat the thread and coming out from under a table young
mum and young dad and I know who that is it must be
time to perform and I stretch out a hand but not a hand I
recognize perhaps it's tentringer's hand and I touch time
I touch the thread of marching time I twang it listen the
thread of marching time is elastic in my o-oringy coat
I've got it this is the job here's the commission
YOU'VE GOT TO GET HOLD OF THE THREAD OF

MARCHING TIME AND PULL THE FUCK
THING DOWN AND GET ON IT AND PANG
YOURSELF TO THE INFINITUDE OF ABSOLUTE
MIND.

[END]